Sun Tzu

THE ART OF WAR

Sun Tzu said:

"The greatest victory is that which requires no battle."

Original title: 孫子兵 法

President: Paulo Roberto Houch
MTB 0083982/SP

Editorial Coordination: Paola Houch and Priscilla Sipans
Art Coordination: Rubens Martim
Translation: Francine Cervato
English text review: Francine Oliveira
Layout: Rogério Pires
Review: Suely Furukawa
Text Preparation: Fabio Kataoka

Sales: Phone: +55 (11) 3393-7727 (comercial2@editoraonline.com.br)

The legal deposit was made.
Printed by PlenaPrint.
1st Print 2025

International Data of Cataloging in Publication (CIP) according to ISBD

C181a Camelot Editora

The Art of War / Camelot Editora. – Barueri : Camelot Editora, 2024.
80 p. ; 15,1cm x 23cm.
Translation of: A Arte da Guerra

ISBN: 978-65-6095-149-5

1. Military Science. 2. Strategy. 3. War. I. Title.

2024-3439 CDD 355.021
CDU 355.01

Elaborated by Vagner Rodolfo da Silva - CRB-8/9410

IBC – Instituto Brasileiro de Cultura LTDA
CNPJ 04.207.648/0001-94
Avenida Juruá, 762 – Alphaville Industrial
ZIP CODE: 06455-010 – Barueri/SP
www.editoraonline.com.br

Summary

Introduction.......... 7

Chapter I
始計 **Laying Plans** **9**

Chapter II
作戰 **Waging War**.......... **13**

Chapter III
謀攻 **Attack by Stratagem**.......... **17**

Chapter IV
軍行 **Tactical Dispositions** **21**

Chapter V
兵勢 **Energy** **26**

Chapter VI
虛實 **Weak Points And Strong**.......... **30**

Chapter VII
軍爭 **Maneuvering**.......... **36**

Chapter VIII
九變 **Variation in Tactics** **43**

Chapter IX
行軍 **The Army on March** **48**

Chapter X
地形 **Terrain**.......... **55**

Chapter XI
九地 **The Nine Situations** **60**

Chapter XII
火攻 **The Attack by Fire** **72**

Chapter XIII
用間 **The Use of Spies** **76**

Statue of Sun Tzu in Yurihama, Tottori, Japan.

INTRODUCTION

The Art of War is considered the best strategy book of all time. Experts claim that this treaty inspired Napoleon, Machiavelli, Mao Tse-Tung, and many other historical personalities.

More than 2,500 years later, the principles attributed to Sun Tzu are still followed nowadays in the world of business, sports, politics, diplomacy, psychology, and personal behavior.

It is a study of the knowledge of human nature in moments of confrontation. The book is not limited to war. It is a work to understand the roots of a conflict and to indicate a solution.

Sun Tzu's work was first released to the West in the period before the French Revolution through a summary translation by the Jesuit priest Joseph-Marie Amiot.

Sun Tzu's concepts arrived in Japan a long time ago, where they were studied by the famous samurai Miyamoto Musashi, who was inspired by him when writing *The Book of Five Rings*.

Some historians concluded that Sun Tzu lived around 500 BC, in the present-day province of Shandong, China. The term "tzu" corresponds to an honorific title used at that time to designate wise men and is equivalent to teacher or master. However, other researchers guarantee that Sun Tzu is not a single person, but rather several Chinese philosophers from that period, who came together to draw up the treaty.

"The greatest victory is that which requires no battle," Sun Tzu said.

The initial text of The Art of War in the classic bamboo book.

CHAPTER I

始計

Laying Plans

Sun Tzu said:

> "The art of war is of vital importance to the state. Under no circumstances can it be neglected."

There are five constant factors that should be the subject of continuous meditation:

- The Moral Law.
- Heaven.
- Earth.
- The Commander.
- Method and Discipline.

The **Moral Law** is what makes the people live in harmony with their ruler, so that they follow it wherever it goes, without fearing for their lives, without fearing exposing themselves to any danger.

Heaven means night and day, cold and heat, time and seasons.

Earth comprises distances, great or small. It indicates danger and safety or open ground and narrow passes, and also the chances of life and death.

The **Commander** represents the virtues of wisdom, sincerity, kindness, courage, and strictness.

Method and discipline indicate the marshaling of the army in its proper subdivisions, the graduations of rank among the officers, the maintenance of roads by which supplies may reach the army, and the control of military expenditure.

These five constant factors need to be known by every commander. Whoever leads soldiers into battle must be familiar with these five factors. Whoever understands them can achieve victory. Whoever does not understand them will be defeated.

Questions that should be asked:

1. Which of the two sovereigns is imbued with the Moral Law?
2. Which of the two generals has the most ability?
3. With whom lie the advantages derived from Heaven and Earth?
4. On which side is discipline most rigorously enforced?
5. Which army is stronger?
6. On which side are officers and men more highly trained?
7. In which army is there greater constancy, both in reward and punishment?

If we consider these factors wisely, we can predict the outcome of a battle.

The commander who takes these questions or stratagems into account will win the battles and remain at the head of his troops. Otherwise, he will suffer defeats and be dismissed.

Deception

All warfare is based on deception.

Hence, when able to attack, we must seem unable; when using our forces, we must seem inactive; when we are near, we must make the enemy believe we are far away; when far away, we must make him believe we are near.

A good leader must:

- Offer bait to entice the enemy, who is looking for some advantage.
- Capture the enemy when he is confused.
- Strengthen itself to face the enemy if he is powerful.

If the opponent:

- Is of choleric temper, seek to irritate it;
- Is humble, encourage his arrogance;
- Is taking his ease, give him no rest;
- Forces are united, separate them.

A military commander must attack where the enemy is unprepared and must use ways that, for the enemy, are unexpected.

These tactics are the key to victory for strategists. However, these factors cannot be determined randomly, based only on situations that occurred in past wars.

The commander must be able to consider all these details and many calculations in advance. Thus, many calculations lead to victory, and few calculations to defeat: it is much worse with no calculation at all!

Illustration by André Castaigne.

CHAPTER II

作戰

Waging War

Sun Tzu said:

"In the operations of war, where there are in the field a thousand swift chariots, as many heavy chariots, and a hundred thousand mail-clad soldiers."

Seek to achieve a quick victory in military operations. If you delay in actions, weapons will be worn out, provisions will be insufficient, and troops will be demoralized. A long battle numbs the army and dampens the spirit and enthusiasm of the soldiers. If you siege a fortified city, your strength will be exhausted. If your army is kept on campaign for a long time, the state's resources will be insufficient.

There is more: when your forces are worn out, with insufficient provisions, demoralized troops, and exhausted resources, neighboring governments will take advantage of this situation and gain leverage to attack you. And you, in this case, even with the most illustrious and wise advisors, will not be able to guarantee a good result in the battle.

Thus, though we have heard of hasty and reckless campaigns, we never had an example of the benefit of prolonging hostilities. There is no instance of a country having benefited from prolonged warfare.

One who does not understand the inherent dangers of military operations is not deeply aware of how to take advantage of it.

An efficient commander does not make a second draft or load his supply wagons more than twice. Once war is declared, he will not waste precious time waiting for reinforcements, nor will he return with his army in search of fresh supplies, but will cross the enemy border without delay. The value of time is greater than numerical superiority or the most perfect calculations regarding supply.

The costs of war

When it sends its troops to wage war in a distant location, the state generally ends up impoverished. Keeping an army away is expensive. Where this army is stationed, the prices of goods will rise; and the high price will exhaust the state's financial resources. When the state's resources are running out, taxes will tend to increase to raise more resources.

Many provisions will be needed for this force to cover a distance of one thousand li (one thousand li = 100 km = 62.1 miles). It will spend a thousand gold bars per day for state expenses and on the battlefield, including envoys abroad and advisors. It will also need materials such as glue, paint, and armor.

All the strength of the state will be consumed on the battlefield. In the end, seventy percent of the people's wealth will be consumed, and sixty percent of the state's income will be wasted, with broken chariots, horses out of action, damaged weapons, including armor and helmets, bows and arrows, spears and shields, herds, and provision wagons.

Obtaining provisions

Consequently, a wise commander must strive to obtain provisions on enemy land. Consuming 20 pounds of enemy food is equivalent to

400 pounds of one's own and 100 pounds of enemy forage is equivalent to one ton of one's own.

Management of the patrimony and captured assets.

If you want to kill the enemy, you have to arouse the hatred of your soldiers; if you want to obtain the enemy's wealth, you have to know how to manage the distribution of the patrimony.

If your army captures ten chariots in a battle, you have to reward the first one who takes the enemy's chariot to you.

Replace the flags of the enemy with your own flags, and mix captured chariots with yours.

At the same time, the captured soldiers should be kindly treated.

Military operations must be driven to a quick victory.

So, the leader who is versed in the art of war becomes the sovereign who can determine the fate of the people and control the safety of the nation.

Illustration by T. Miyano.

CHAPTER III

謀攻

Attack by Stratagem

Sun Tzu said:

"In the practical art of war, the best thing of all is to take the enemy's country whole and intact; to shatter and destroy it is not so good. So, too, it is better to capture an army entire than to destroy it, to capture a regiment, a detachment or a company entire than to destroy them."

Invincibility is in oneself; vulnerability is in the opponent.

Start by dominating a battalion, a company, or a squadron of five men.

To fight and conquer in all your battles is not supreme excellence; supreme excellence consists in breaking the enemy's resistance without fighting.

Policy for military operations

The best policy for military operations is to achieve victory by attacking the enemy's strategy. The second-best policy is to disintegrate the enemy's alliances through diplomacy and then attack its soldiers, launching an offensive on the enemy. The worst policy is to violently attack fortified cities and subjugate territories.

- Attack strategies
- Attack alliances
- Attack soldiers

Attacks on cities

Besieging cities is a tactic that should only be used as a last resort. It is a time-consuming operation, which can take approximately three months. It will be necessary to build protected stairs, prepare vehicles, and gather sufficient equipment and weapons. Then, it will take another three months to prepare earthen ramps to reach the city walls.

If the commander cannot control his own anxiety and orders his soldiers to move against the city wall like ants, the result will be that 1/3 of them will be sacrificed while the city remains untouched. In fact, there lies the calamity in attacking walled cities.

Win without fighting

A leader who is well-versed in military operations makes the enemy surrender without fighting, and captures the enemy's cities without attacking them violently. And destroys the enemy's state without lengthy military operations.

The greatest prize of a victory is to triumph through stratagems without using troops.

How to use troops

Thus, the law for using troops is:

- When you have ten times the enemy's forces, surround them;
- If your forces exceed the enemy's by five times, attack them;
- When you have twice as many forces as the enemy, face them on both sides;
- If your forces are equivalent, try to divide those of the enemy;
- If your forces are inferior, be skilled at taking the defensive;
- If you are much weaker than the enemy, you must know when to withdraw;
- If the weakest fights without considering this ratio of forces, he will certainly be conquered by the strongest.

The value of the commander

The commander is the balance of the state chariot. If this balance is well-placed, the chariot, that is, the nation, will be powerful; if the balance is faulty, the nation will certainly be weak.

There are three ways in which a ruler can bring misfortune to its own army:

Firstly, if he orders an advance and his army cannot move forward, or issues orders for a withdrawal, unaware that his army cannot withdraw.

Then, if he interferes with the administrative part of the army, without understanding the internal affairs, he will confuse the officers and soldiers.

Thirdly, when he interferes with the operational part of the army without knowing the principles of military stratagems, he will generate doubts and disagreements between officers and soldiers.

With the commander confusing his army and losing the trust of his men, aggression from neighboring states will not take long.

Therein lies the meaning of the expression: "To throw disorder and confusion into one's own ranks is to offer a sure way to the enemy's victory."

Which opponent will be the winner?

The one who knows when to fight or when not to fight.

The one who knows how to adopt the appropriate military art according to the superiority or inferiority of his forces against the enemy.

The one who knows how to keep his superiors and subordinates united according to his proposals.

The one who is well prepared and faces an unprepared enemy.

The one who is a wise and capable commander, whose sovereign leader does not interfere in his decisions.

The one who knows the enemy and himself will fight a hundred battles without weakening.

For the one who does not know the enemy, but knows himself, the chances of victory or defeat will be equal.

The one who does not know either the enemy or himself will be defeated in every battle.

CHAPTER IV

軍行

Tactical Dispositions

Sun Tzu said:

> "To secure ourselves against defeat lies in our own hands, but the opportunity of defeating the enemy is provided by the enemy himself."

There are three ways for a ruler to bring disgrace to his army:

1. Demanding the armed force to advance or retreat without caring if this demand cannot be obeyed. This is called hindering the army.
2. Trying to command an army in the same way as managing the kingdom, ignoring the conditions that prevail in the army. Opportunism and flexibility are military virtues.
3. Ignoring the military principle of adapting to circumstances. This shakes soldiers' confidence.

Old skilled warriors first put themselves beyond the possibility of defeat and then waited for an opportunity to defeat the enemy.

The warrior wins battles by making no mistakes. Making no mistakes is what establishes the certainty of victory, for it means conquering an enemy that is already defeated.

Attack and defense

When there is no chance of victory, take a defensive position. When there is a chance of victory, launch an attack.

If favorable conditions are insufficient, you must defend yourself; if favorable conditions are abundant, you should make an attack.

The defense expert hides himself, even underground. The attack expert strikes the enemy from the topmost heights of heaven. Thus, he is capable of protecting himself and gaining victory.

Conditions for a victory

The predictability of a victory does not exceed the common sense of common people.

A victory that is won after a fierce battle and is universally praised is not the apogee of excellence, just as the raising of a strand of hair is not a sign of strength, just as seeing the sun and the moon is not a sign of sharp sight, nor is hearing thunder a gift of acute hearing.

The ancients said that the expert in the art of war won when victory was easily predictable. Thus, a battle won by an expert does not earn a reputation for wisdom or credit for courage.

The expert's victories are infallible, as he only fights when the enemy is already defeated, and he is destined for defeat.

Therefore, the strategist occupies an invincible position, and, at the same time, he is sure not to miss any military opportunity to defeat the enemy.

Thus, a victorious army will not fight the enemy until it is certain of the victory conditions, while a defeated army begins the battle and hopes to gain victory afterward.

The expert always understands the principles of war and adopts the correct policies, so that victory will always be in his hands.

Important elements in the art of war

Five important details of military rules must be followed:

- First: the analysis of the environment;
- Second: the calculation of human and material resources;
- Third: the calculation of logistics capacity;
- Fourth: a comparison of his own military forces with that of the enemy;
- Fifth: a prediction of victory or defeat.

Application of military rules

An excellent commander will have the wisdom to understand that:

- The physical characteristics of a battlefield must be verified along with the assessment of the environment;
- The calculation of the workforce and material resources is used to estimate the quantity of resources;
- Logistics capacity must meet provisional needs;
- In the balance of power, one of the weights is based on logistics capacity;
- The possibility of victory is based on the balance of power.

A victorious army is like a weight of 200 pounds against one weighing just a few grams, while a defeated army is like a weight of a few grams compared to a few hundred pounds. The first one has an obvious advantage over the second one.

A commander who uses all that weight and launches his men into battle and obtains victory will be compared to the force of dammed waters that fall from a height of ten thousand feet.

Warriors of Xian, a collection of terracotta sculptures representing the armies of Qin Shi Huang, the first emperor of China.

CHAPTER V

兵勢

Energy

Sun Tzu said:

"The control of a large force is the same principle as the control of a few men: it is merely a question of dividing up their numbers.

Fighting with a large army under your command is nowise different from fighting with a small one: it is merely a question of instituting signs and signals."

Making an entire army capable of resisting an attack without suffering defeat depends on the correct application of military tactics.

By adopting frontal or surprise tactics, a commander ensures that his army does not suffer defeats against the enemy.

Discovering strong and weak points allows the army to fall on its enemy like a stone on an egg.

Tactics

During a war, the commander must adopt overt tactics to confront the enemy and must use intelligence tactics if he wants to achieve victory.

Illustration by Tsukioka Yoshitoshi

The commander, by applying intelligence tactics, becomes as infinite as heaven and earth, and as the endless flow of a river. Just like the sun and the moon, he stops and then starts again, like the movement of nature.

There are only five musical notes, but their combinations produce the most pleasant and wonderful melodies we hear. There are only five basic colors, but when combined, they produce the most beautiful and splendid colors we see. There are only five flavors, but mixing them together produces the most delicious tastes we can taste.

Let's remember that in ancient China, there were five musical notes, which were: gong, shang, jue, zhi, and yu; five basic colors – blue, yellow, red, white, and black; and five cardinal flavors – sour, salty, acrid, bitter, and sweet.

This is what military operations are like; there are only overt and intelligence operations, but their variations and combinations will give rise to an infinite series of maneuvers. Overt and intelligence tactics are mutually dependent, and they are like a cyclical movement that has neither a beginning nor an end. Who knows its infinity?

Advantages and opportunities

A fast-flowing torrent can bounce heavy rocks from the riverbed because of the strong push of the water.

A hawk that flies so fast when it strikes can destroy its prey, due to the opportunity and rapidity of its attack.

It is the same with a commander, who can explore his own advantage position and launch a quick, sharp attack. His potential is like a bow, fully stretched, which launches, at the precise moment, the right arrow. In the turmoil of a battle, his army remains calm. In the chaos of a war, where positions are constantly changing, it remains invulnerable.

Exploring the advantages

Disorder is born from order; cowardice comes from courage; and weakness is born from strength. Order and disorder depend on organization and logistics; courage and cowardice depend on circumstances or strategic advantage; strength and weakness depend on dispositions.

So, if the commander wants the enemy to move, he shows himself. The enemy will certainly follow him. If he wants to attract the enemy, he deceives, presenting something profitable element for the enemy, and the enemy will certainly believe in it. Thus, the commander offers the enemy small advantages, but awaits it armed and with all his forces.

A skilled leader in warfare explores his strategic advantage and does not ask for it from his men. Therefore, this commander must know how to select the right men and explore a favorable situation.

The one who explores strategic advantage leads his men as if they were logs or stones. The nature of logs or stones is to remain impassive if the ground is flat; or roll if the ground is sloping; if they are square, they tend to stop; if they are round, they tend to roll.

Thus, the commander's strategic advantage can be compared to a round stone rolling down a steep mountain of ten thousand feet. This is the meaning of strategic advantage.

CHAPTER VI

虛實

Weak Points And Strong

Sun Tzu said:

"Whoever is first in the field and awaits the coming of the enemy, will be fresh for the fight; whoever is second in the field and has to hasten to battle will arrive exhausted."

Therefore the clever combatant imposes his will on the enemy, but does not allow the enemy's will to be imposed on him.

Present an apparent advantage to the enemy and he will come to your trap. Threaten him with some danger and you can stop it.

So, the commander's skill consists of tiring the enemy when he is rested; making him hungry when he has provisions; forcing him to move if he is quietly encamped.

Exploring vulnerabilities

A commander and his troops can march a distance of a thousand *li* without getting tired because the march takes place in an area where the enemy has not set up his defenses.

Illustration by Tsukioka Yoshitoshi

If a commander attacks with confidence, it is because he knows that the enemy cannot defend himself or strengthen his position. If a commander defends with confidence, it is because he is sure that the enemy will not attack with superior forces in that position.

Thus, against the attack expert, the enemy does not know where to defend himself. On the other hand, against a defense expert, the enemy does not know where to attack.

It is important to be extremely subtle, so subtle that no one can find any trace of him.

He must be extremely mysterious, so mysterious that no one can hear any information about him.

If a commander can act like this, then he can keep the enemy's fate in his own hands.

The enemy will not be able to resist your attack if you attack his weak points.

When retreating, you cannot be pursued because, moving so quickly, the enemy will not be able to pursue or reach you.

Dominating the will of the enemy

When we decide to attack, the enemy will have no choice, even defending himself with high walls and deep moats. He will be compelled to fight because he was attacked, and he must defend himself.

If we decide not to fight against him, we will not do that, because even if our defense is just a drawn line, we will divert it to another objective.

If we can make the enemy reveal his position while we are hiding ours, we can gather our troops and divide that of the enemy.

If we concentrate our forces in one place, while the enemy disperses his own forces in ten places, then we will be ten against one when we launch our attack.

If we have to use many to attack a few, then it will be quite easy to negotiate, as the enemy will be small and weak.

Forcing the enemy to take precautions

The place our forces intend to attack must not be known to the enemy. In this way, if he cannot predict the location of our attack, he will have to take precautions in many places, and when he takes precautions in many places, his troops will be few in number, wherever that may be.

- If the enemy strengthen his van, he will weaken his rear;
- Should he strengthen his rear, he will weaken his van;
- Should he strengthen his left, he will weaken his right;
- Should he strengthen his right, he will weaken his left.
- If he sends reinforcements everywhere, he will everywhere be weak.

The one who has few forces must take precautions everywhere against possible attacks; the one who has many troops compels the enemy to prepare against his attacks.

Knowing the time and place of the battle

If a commander knows the place and time of a battle, he can lead his troops up to a thousand li, even for a decisive battle. If he knows neither the place nor the time of a battle, then his left side cannot help his right, and his right wing cannot save his left; the front troops cannot help the rear troops, nor can the rear troops help the front troops. And so it will be, regardless of whether the troops are a few meters or tens of miles away.

Determining the situation of the enemy

Although the (enemy) troops are very numerous, how can this help you achieve a victory for your side?

Victory can be created. Even if the enemy troops are many, we can find a way to make them unable to fight.

Consider and analyze the situation of the enemy and where he wants to fight, so you can have a clear understanding of your chances of success.

Determine his attack and defense patterns, and discover his vulnerable points. By counting the number of soldiers and horses, you can know the size of the troop and their weak points.

Perform combats of minor importance to determine where the enemy is strong and where it is vulnerable.

The gift of military art

The most important gift of the military art of deceiving the enemy is hiding your intentions. Thus, even the enemy's most penetrating spies will not be able to spy, and not even the wisest man will be able to conspire against you.

Even if you make public the tactics that led to your victories, they will not be understood. Although everyone knows your winning tactics, they will never be able to learn how you came to define the advantageous position that led you to victory.

Victories in battle can never be repeated. The circumstances of each fight are unique and require their own particular response.

Military tactics are like running water

Military tactics are like running water. Running water always moves from top to bottom, avoids high ground and flows to low ground. The military tactics are this way: they always avoid the strong points of the enemy and attack his weak points.

Just as the river changes its course according to the accidents of the ground, the army varies its methods of obtaining victory according to the enemy.

In the same way that water does not maintain its constant shape, there are no constant conditions in war, either.

The one who directs military operations with great skill can obtain victory by employing appropriate tactics according to the different situations of the enemy. Just like the five elements (metal, wood, water, fire, and earth), where none is exclusively predominant, the four seasons, where none of them last forever; the days that are sometimes long, sometimes short; and the moon, which sometimes grows and sometimes wanes.

CHAPTER VII

軍爭

Maneuvering

Sun Tzu said:

"In war, the general receives his commands from the sovereign. Having collected an army and concentrated his forces, he must blend and harmonize the different elements thereof before pitching his camp. After that, comes tactical maneuvering, than which there is nothing more difficult."

The secret lies in transforming the deviation into a straight line, the misfortune into an advantage. Thus, taking a long and tortuous road, after having lured the enemy out of it, even if you left after him, managing to reach the objective before.

It is hard because it is about transforming a tortuous path into a straight road, transforming a disadvantage into an advantage.

Illustration by Utagawa Kuniyoshi

A good strategist can deceive the enemy, taking him on a tortuous route, offering easy advantages, and causing the enemy to arrive later and be surprised.

Dangers of military maneuver

There are not only advantages to the maneuver, but also dangers.

If you strive to occupy a favorable position in a battle and lead the entirety of your forces, naturally, you will have your speed reduced. If, however, you leave your troops, equipment, and provisions behind, this will be lost.

Thus, if your army, to gain an advantage, had to collect its armor and leave its positions quickly, carrying out a forced march of a thousand li, without stopping day or night, your main commanders would be captured; your strongest and most vigorous men would arrive first, and the weak and tired ones would stray. And, in this way, only 1/10 of the army would arrive on time.

If they had to run fifty li to look for a favorable position, the vanguard commander would be lost, and only half the army would get there on time.

If they had to run thirty li to fight for some advantage, only 2/3 would arrive. Everyone knows that an army will be defeated by the enemy if it does not have equipment, provisions, or support material.

Full knowledge

A leader who does not understand the intentions, plots and schemes of the rulers of neighboring states cannot form alliances with them.

A leader who is not familiar with the topographical characteristics of different mountains and forests, of dirty grounds and swamps, cannot manage the march of an army.

A leader who does not hire local guides cannot gain a favorable position on the ground for the battle.

The art of maneuvering armies

In military operations, you can achieve victory with military stratagems. You must maneuver to obtain favorable conditions and disperse or concentrate the army according to the circumstances.

A good strategist must be:

- As fast as the strong wind, when he comes into action;
- As stable as the silent forests that the wind cannot shake when moving slowly;
- As fierce and violent as the raging flames, when invading the enemy state;
- As steady as the high mountains, when stationing
- As inscrutable as something behind the clouds and striking as suddenly as thunder;

He must divide his forces to plunder the enemy's territory, and position them in strategic locations to defend the recently captured territory.

He must weigh the advantages and disadvantages before going into battle.

The one who first masters this tactic will gain victory. This is the art of maneuvering armies.

To manage a large army

An old book about war from the time of Sun Tzu says that the spoken word does not go far enough, which is why the use of gongs and drums is recommended. Not even common objects can be seen clearly enough, hence the institution of banners and flags.

Gongs and drums, banners, and flags are means by which the ears and eyes of the host may be focused on a specific point.

If vision and hearing converge simultaneously on the same object, the evolutions of up to a million soldiers will be like those of a single man.

In the night fight, then, make much use of signal fires and drums, and in the day fight, of flags and standards, as a means of influencing the ears and eyes of your army.

Rule for managing morale

You can demoralize the enemy and make the commander lose spirit. Normally, at the beginning of war, the enemy's spirit is acute and irresistible. After a certain period, it will recede and relax. In the final stages of the war, it will become weak, and the soldiers will be in no mood to fight.

The skillful leader always avoids the enemy when his morale is high and irresistible, and attacks when he is tired and reluctant to fight. This is the rule for managing morale.

Rule for controlling military force

The leader takes his troops close to the battlefield to wait for the enemy that comes from afar; he leads his rested troops against the exhausted enemy, and brings his well-fed troops against the enemy soldiers that are hungry. This is the rule for controlling military force.

Mutable conditions of tactics

The skilled leader never faces an enemy who lines up in perfect, united order with aligned and high flags, nor does he attack an enemy who adopts a strong and impressive battle formation. This shows that he has a clear understanding of mutable conditions of tactics.

Principles of military maneuvers

Some principles of military maneuvers:

The Battle of Wafanghou. Illustration by Hermanus Willem Koekkoek

1. Never launch an attack on an enemy that occupies high ground.
2. Do not attack the enemy when there are hills that support him.
3. Do not chase an enemy who pretends to retreat.
4. Neither attack enemy forces that are rested and strong.
5. Never take a bait offered by the enemy, nor obstruct the enemy who withdraws from the front.
6. For a surrounded enemy, you must leave a way to the exit; and do not press too hard on an enemy who is desperate in a corner with no way out.

Such is the art of war.

CHAPTER VIII

九變

Variation in Tactics

Sun Tzu said:

> "The general who thoroughly understands the advantages that accompany variation of tactics knows how to handle his troops."

Military tactics

When leading his troops, he must not camp or station in difficult ground; he must ally himself with the rulers of places where the road is strategically important; he should not linger on open ground; he must be prepared with cunning and stratagems when penetrating ground subject to ambush; he must fight very aggressively on a ground from which there is no way to advance or to withdraw.

A commander must clearly understand these tactics. If he understands them, then he knows about military operations. If he does not have a clear understanding of the real values of these tactics, he will not know how to use them in his favor, even if he is familiar with the topography of the ground where the battle will take place.

If a commander does not know these tactical variables, he will not be able to get the most out of his soldiers, even if he knows the five advantages.

There are some roads that should not be travelled; and enemies that should not be attacked. There are some cities that should not be captured, some territories that should not be contested, and some orders from the sovereign that do not need to be obeyed.

Weighing advantages and disadvantages

A wise commander must take advantages and disadvantages into account. Knowing the advantages, he will be successful in his plans. Knowing the disadvantages, he will be able to solve the difficulties.

If you want to subdue neighboring states, threaten them with what they fear; if you want to keep them as servants, use coercion; if you want to deceive the enemy, offer him small advantages..

In military operations, this is a useful rule: "Never rely on the probability that the enemy is not on the way, but depend on your own readiness to recognize it. Do not hope that the enemy does not attack, but depend on being in a position where you cannot be attacked."

Fatal weaknesses of a commander

There are five fatal weaknesses of a commander:

1. If he is brave and has a disregard for life, he could be easily killed.
2. If he is a coward on the eve of a battle, he will be easily captured.
3. If he has an angry temper, he will be easily provoked.;
4. If he is too susceptible to honor, he will be liable to be shamed.
5. If he is very benevolent and values people, he will be liable to become hesitant and passive.

These five weaknesses must be carefully observed and avoided. It is the fault of a commander that can prove fatal in the conduct of a war.

The destruction of the entire army and the deaths of the leaders are the inevitable results of these five fatal weaknesses.

Reproduction of part of a folding screen depicting the Genpei Warsde uma tela dobrável que retrata as Guerras Genpei.

CHAPTER IX

行軍

The Army on March

Sun Tzu said:

"In military art and good troop management, there are, in general, only two types of things: those that are done in secret and those that are done openly. But in practice, it is a chain of operations whose end we do not know; it is like a moving wheel that has no beginning or end."

Regarding the positioning of the army

Take the names of all the officers, both superior and minor, and write them down in a separate catalog, with a note of the talents and capabilities of each one, in order to be able to employ them with advantage if the occasion presents itself, so all those under your command will be persuaded that your main concern is to protect them from any danger.

Regarding mountains

A commander must observe the following: when passing by mountains, he must try to be safe, staying close to the valleys; select a place on high ground that receives sunlight to carry out military camps; and not climb to reach the enemy. This is the rule for positioning regarding the mountains.

Regarding rivers

After crossing a river, you must stay away from it. If the enemy attacks come from a river, do not face them in the water. Instead, it is advantageous to allow half the troops to cross it, and then strike them. If you wish to fight with the enemy, do not face their invasion forces near a river. Instead, select a place on high ground that receives sunlight to take up the position, and never camp in the direction of the enemy's stream. This is the rule for positioning regarding rivers.

Regarding salt marshes

Cross the salt marshes quickly and without delay. When encountering enemy troops in a salt marsh, position yourself near the grass with your back to the forest. This is the rule for positioning regarding salt marshes.

Regarding flat lands

In flat lands, select an accessible place, position yourself with your right flank, a high field at your back, dangerous land in front, and safe ground in your rear. This is the rule for positioning regarding flat lands.

These are the same four useful rules that allowed the Yellow Emperor to defeat four emperors (leaders of four tribes in the Yellow Emperor's time).

Advantages offered by the ground

All commanders prefer to station their troops on high ground rather than low ground; they prefer sunlight rather than shade; and where crops can grow and the soil is protected. The troops will be free from disease, and this will guarantee victory.

When encountering hills or dikes, you should station your troops on the sunny side, with the hills or dikes in your rear. These advantages are offered by the ground, and it is up to the commander to know how to use them.

Precautions with nature

If heavy rain falls on the upper parts of a river and forms torrents that rush to the lower parts, do not cross the river, but wait until the waters calm down.

When you find yourself in dangerous areas, never approach them, and avoid them quickly: a gorge with a river running at the bottom; a ravine, with dangerous precipices all around; soils densely covered with high woods; a marshy land; and a narrow pass between two mountains.

Stay away from these positions and let the enemy approach them; by keeping them in front of us, we will be able to maneuver, and the enemy will have them in the rear.

If the army has on its flanks steep ravines, swamps, and reeds, or wooded mountains with dense vegetation, you must carefully and repeatedly examine them to see if there are no ambushes, or if someone is spying.

Signs

Positioning of enemy troops:

- If enemy troops are close to your positions and remain quiet, it is because the position is not advantageous to them.
- If enemy troops are far from you and still dare to come and challenge you to battle, it is because they want to seduce you to make an advance.
- If enemy troops are on flat land, it is because there are practical advantages to this position.

Evidence from nature

- If the trees are moving, the enemy is advancing towards you.
- If you find many obstacles hidden among the undergrowth, the enemy is trying to confuse you.
- If birds take flight, the enemy is waiting for an ambush.
- Birds that gather over the camp area of the enemy suggest that the camp must be abandoned and that the enemy ran away.
- Frightened animals, which run away, indicate a sign of an imminent attack by the enemy.
- Dust clouds rising high indicate that enemy chariots are approaching. When the dust settles and spreads across the ground, it is a sign that enemy infantry is arriving. But if the dust is raised in isolated spots, then the enemy is chopping wood for the fires. Dust that is low and rises intermittently indicates that the enemy is setting up camps.

Negotiations

- If the messenger of the enemy speaks moderate words, but the war preparations continue, he will advance.
- When the enemy speaks bellicosely and threatens to advance, he will withdraw.
- If the enemy sends a messenger with conciliatory words, it is because he wishes for a truce.
- When the enemy calls for a truce but he did not suffer a setback, then he is up to something.

Enemy formations

- When the light chariots of the enemy leave first and take up positions on the wings, it means that the enemy is organizing his battle formation.

- When enemy commanders become busy and move to organize the positions of soldiers, on foot and in armed vehicles, then the enemy is waiting to launch a decisive attack.
- When half of the enemy troops advance and the other half retreat, it means the enemy is trying to attract us to a trap.

Enemy behavior

- When the soldiers of the enemy lean on their own weapons, you will deduce that they are hungry and fatigued.
- When the soldiers that bring water drink it first, it means that the enemy has suffered from thirst.
- If soldiers gather in small groups, whisper, and everyone complains, it is because the commander lost their support.
- When more officers become irritable, the enemy is tired of war.

Enemy in disarray

- And if there is an advantage and the enemy does not try to obtain it, it is because the enemy is completely exhausted.
- At night, screams are heard in the enemy's camp; it is because the troops are afraid and insecure.
- When there is disarray in the enemy's camp, it means that its commanders have lost prestige and authority.
- When flags and banners constantly change positions, the enemy is in disarray.
- If the enemy feeds his horses with grain and his soldiers with meat, when he destroys his cooking utensils and shows no intention of returning to camp, it means that he is desperate and will fight to the death.

Rewards

- A commander who excessively rewards his soldiers is in trouble.
- The one who punishes his soldiers a lot is in serious distress.
- If he treats his soldiers with violence and then fears that they will betray him, he is extremely inept.
- If you punish soldiers who are not yet devoted to you, they will not obey you, and if they do not obey you, it will be difficult to use them. But even with the devotion of the troops, if strict and impartial discipline is not reinforced, you will also have no way of using them.
- Thus, you must command your troops with civility and humanity, to keep your men united; and with martial discipline, to keep them in line. This will ensure loyalty, and you will be invincible.
- If orders are constantly reinforced, soldiers will be obedient; otherwise, they will be disobedient.
- If orders are constantly reinforced, there will be a complementary relationship of trust between the commander and his men.
- An enemy who confronts you for a long time without fighting or abandoning his position must be considered with the greatest care.
- What is enough is: being able to assess your own strength, have a clear vision of the enemy's situation, and obtain full support from your men. The one who does not make plans or strategies, and belittles the enemy, will surely be captured by the opponent.

CHAPTER X

地形

Terrain

Sun Tzu said:

"We may distinguish six kinds of terrain, to wit: (1) Accessible ground; (2) entangling ground; (3) temporizing ground; (4) narrow passes; (5) precipitous heights; (6) positions at a great distance from the enemy."

Types of ground

What is an accessible ground? It is the one that appears easy for both your troops and those of the enemy. If you enter an accessible region, you must occupy high, sunny positions, and keep your supply lines clear. So, it will be convenient for you to fight with the enemy.

What is entangling ground? It is the one that is easy for you to enter, but hard to leave. On this ground, if you encounter the enemy and he is off guard, then you will defeat him. However, if the enemy is prepared and if you launch an attack, not only can you be defeated but you will also have difficult ground to retreat from. This is the disadvantage of this type of ground.

What is a temporising ground? It is the one that proves difficult for both the enemy and your troops. In a temporising terrain, even if the enemy tries to attract you to fight, you must not take the bait but pretend that you are in withdrawal. When enemy troops are halfway in pursuit of you, you can strike them. This is the advantage of a temporising ground.

What is narrow passes? It is the one that presents a valley between two mountains. If you occupy this type of ground, you must block the narrow passages with strong garrisons and wait for the enemy. If the enemy occupied this ground before and blocked these narrow passages, you must not pursue it. If the enemy did not block these passages, you can search for them.

What is precipitous heights? It is the one that contains rivers, mountains, cliffs, hills, and ridges. If you reach high, precipitous heights before the enemy, you must take a high position on the sunny side and wait for the enemy that is approaching. If the enemy forces control this type of ground, you must withdraw your troops and not pursue them.

What is a position at a great distance from the enemy? It is the one that presents considerable distances between the opposing camps. In this type of ground, if the advantages of your troops and enemy troops are equivalent, it will certainly not be easy to attract the enemy into a battle. Likewise, it will be disadvantageous to take the battle to it.

These are the ways to take advantage of the six different types of ground to fight on. Commanders have the highest responsibility to investigate them carefully.

Six situations that point to the defeat of an army

A commander must know the six situations that point to the defeat of an army:

1. When soldiers run away;
2. When they have negligent discipline;
3. When the army is deteriorated;

4. When they crumble under insurgency;
5. When they are disorganized;
6. When they were defeated.

None of these situations are the result of natural disasters; they are the result of the failures of commanders.

When the strategic advantages are equal between you and your enemy, and if your army has to fight against forces ten times larger, the result will be your escape.

When the soldiers are brave and qualified, but the officers are weak and incompetent, then the entire army will be negligent regarding discipline.

When officers are brave and competent, but soldiers are weak and untrained, the army will deteriorate.

When senior officers have grudges against commanders, they are insubordinate and, when encountering the enemy, will rush into battle without authorization. If, at the same time, the commander is ignorant of their abilities, then the army will fall apart.

When the leader is weak, incompetent, and does not command respect, when officers and soldiers behave in an undisciplined way, when formal training and clear instructions are lacking, and when military formations are disorganized, the army is disorganized.

If a leader does not calculate the forces of the enemy and employs a small force against a large army, fights a strong enemy with weak troops, and at the same time does not select vanguard units, the result will be defeat.

Therefore, these six situations are the causes of defeat. Commanders have the highest responsibility to investigate them carefully.

Basic duties of a commander

In military operations, the ground is an important ally of the commander. Correctly assessing the enemy situation, creating favorable conditions for victory, and analyzing the types of ground and distances very carefully, these are the basic duties of a wise commander.

The one who correctly assesses these aspects and knows how to apply them will win; the one who is ignorant of these rules and does not know how to employ them in war will be defeated.

If, by studying the existing situation and being certain that the outcome of the battle will result in victory, a wise commander will decide to fight, even if the sovereign does not order it to. Conversely, if the situation points to a defeat, it will decide not to fight, even if the sovereign orders it to do so.

If a commander advances without seeking personal fame and retreats without exempting itself from responsibility; if his concern is to protect the population and people's safety and promote the interests of the sovereign, then there is a leader who is like a precious stone of the state.

If the commander cares for his soldiers as if they were children, they will follow it to the deepest places; if he treats them affectionately, as if they were his own beloved children, then they will be willing to die in battle.

If the commander favors his men but does not know how to use them, he arms them, but cannot command them; and when they violate laws and regulations, he does not punish them or call them to order, such soldiers are like spoiled children and will be useless for battle.

Knowing the situation

A commander who only knows the capabilities of his troops, but does not know the invulnerability of the enemy, will only have half the chance of victory.

A commander who knows that the enemy can be defeated, but does not know the inability of his own troops, will also only have half the chance of victory.

A commander who knows that the enemy can be defeated and that his own troops have the capacity to attack, but does not know that the conditions of the ground are unsuitable for battle, will have his chances of victory reduced by half.

Thus, a skilled commander will always move his forces in the right direction and, when he takes action, his resources will be unlimited.

Thus, it is said: “Know the enemy and yourself, and you will gain victory without any danger; know the ground and the conditions of nature, and you will always be victorious.”

CHAPTER XI

九地

The Nine Situations

Sun Tzu said:

"In military operations, the ground can be classified according to nine geographic positions that affect the way military operations are carried out. In this way, the types of ground are as follows: dispersive, facile, contentious, open, ground of intersecting highways, serious, difficult, hemmed, and desperate."

The art of war recognizes nine tactical situations that one may face, depending on the ground.

1. Dispersive: when a ruler undertakes a campaign in his own territory, the place is called dispersive.
2. Facile: enemy territory into which one enters, but does not penetrate deeply, is called facile.

3. Contentious: the territory whose occupation is favorable, both for the enemy and for our forces, is called contentious ground.
4. Open: a ground that is accessible from both sides is called open ground.
5. Ground of intersecting highways: a territory where several neighboring states meet, and which has important intersections, is called ground of intersecting highways. The one who acquires its control first will obtain an alliance with the other neighbors.
6. Serious: when a ruler penetrates deeply into hostile territory, after having crossed many enemy cities, he finds himself in a serious territory.
7. Difficult: a ground with high mountains, dense forests, and impenetrable swamps, or any place where it is difficult to travel is called difficult ground.
8. Hemmed: a ground to which access is narrow, and any return requires a detour, so that a troop, even a small one, will be enough to defeat a large army, is called hemmed ground.
9. Desperate: a ground where only a desperate battle with all your forces will save you, but if you fail, you will be defeated and destroyed, is called desperate ground.

Conduct on different types of ground

Therefore, never fight on a dispersive ground; never remain on a facile ground; never attack an enemy who first reached a contentious ground; never allow army communications to be blocked on open ground; form alliances with rulers of neighboring states on a ground of intersecting highways; plunder the resources of the enemy for your provisions on a hemmed territory; quickly cross difficult grounds; draw up plans and stratagems to cross the hemmed grounds; and fight a battle with all your forces on desperate ground.

Ancient tactics

In the past, qualified commanders in military operations sought to:

- Prevent the enemies' vanguard and rearguard from establishing contact;
- Prevent the enemy's main body and its small divisions from supporting mutually;
- Prevent enemy officers and subordinates from supporting themselves mutually and communicating with each other;
- Disperse enemy soldiers so that they could not gather, and if they gather, so that they could not form groups.

Qualified commanders would advance when the situation is favorable for them and remain stationed when the situation is unfavorable for them.

When asked: "If the enemy comes to attack you with a large, well- ordered army, how would you deal with it?"

The answer is: "Capture something he values, and he will bow to your wishes."

Essence of military operations

The essence of military operations is the speed of actions and the exploration of the vulnerabilities of the enemy, taking paths he does not expect and attacking where he is not prepared.

General principles for waging war in enemy territory

The general principles for waging war in enemy territory are as follows:

The more you penetrate a hostile territory, and your soldiers are cohesive, the more difficult it will be for the defenders to defeat you.

If you penetrate a fertile land, you must plunder the fields of the enemy, as this will guarantee provisions for your men.

Feed your soldiers and do not wear them out; keep their morale high and conserve their energy.

Move your troops with ingenious tactics so that the enemy cannot predict your stratagem.

You must launch your soldiers into situations from which there is no chance of withdrawal and from which they will not run away, not even when facing death.

And when soldiers are not afraid of death, there will be nothing for them to fear, and they will give their all in their battles.

Soldiers that penetrate deep into enemy territory will be fearless, there will be no road for them to withdraw, and they will stand their ground.

Being in enemy territory, they will be cohesive. On this ground, there is no choice, and every fight will be like a desperate battle.

Thus, such soldiers do not need any training to be vigilant. They will do what you want, even before you tell them to; they will cooperate, even before you determine; and they will head towards you consciously, even before you order them to.

You must forbid superstitions and dispel rumors and suspicions among your soldiers, so that they will not abandon the battle, even in the face of death.

Soldiers have no excess wealth because they despise material goods; they do not fear death and do not care about longevity.

On the day the army is ordered to fight a decisive battle, the soldiers will be able to sit down and cry with tears that wet their clothes; some will be able to lie down and cry with tears that flow down their cheeks. But if you launch them into a situation where there is no way for them to withdraw, they will prove fearless and as brave as Zhuan Zhu or Cao Gui.

Research indicates that Zhuan Zhu, without fear of death, attacked the Duke of Huan alone, armed only with a knife, recovering lands that had been taken from him. Cao Gui, a criminal from Wu province, even though he knew he would receive the death penalty, killed King Liao.

The snake of Ch'ang Mountains

Those who are qualified in military operations should be like Shuai-jan, the snake of Ch'ang Mountains. If you hit its head, its tail will launch an attack against you; if you hit its tail, its head will hit you; if you hit its body, it will attack with its head and tail.

If they asked: "Can soldiers achieve this instantaneous coordination like that snake?"

The answer would be: "They can."

Everyone knows that the people of Wu and the people of Yue are enemies, but if they traveled in the same boat caught in a storm, they would help each other, the same way that the left and right hands cooperate.

Tying the legs of war horses or burying chariot wheels in the ground were never reliable ways to keep soldiers together and prevent desertions from combat.

Keeping soldiers engaged in battle and willing to fight courageously depends on good administration and good military command.

The correct exploration of situations will bring courage to soldiers and allow them to explore the possibilities of their troops.

A skilled commander must command thousands and thousands of horses and men as if he was leading a single man, who will not hesitate to follow him.

To command an army

- A commander must have a calm and unfathomable mind.
- He must command his troops in an impartial and vertical way.
- He must keep his officers and soldiers ignorant of his military plans.
- He changes his troop dispositions and military plans without anyone knowing.

- He modifies his camp areas, using different paths, without anyone anticipating his intentions.
- A commander who leads his troops to fight a decisive battle must cut off all means of withdrawal, just as one throws back a ladder after climbing a height.
- When he leads his troops into a neighboring kingdom, he should have the momentum of an arrow that was launched.
- He commands his soldiers just as one does with a flock of sheep, without anyone knowing their destination.
- He gathers his entire army and penetrates dangerous situations with it.

This is what a commander should do.

Tactics vary according to the types of ground, movements of advance or retreat, favorable conditions, and the observation of human nature; it is all that a commander has to study and carefully examine.

Waging war in enemy territory

The deeper your warriors penetrate hostile territory, the greater their fighting spirit will be.

The less deeply your warriors penetrate in hostile territory, the less willing they will be to fight.

When you cross the border into a neighboring country, into a battlefield where there is no way for soldiers to return, you are on serious ground.

By occupying a position that extends in all directions, you entered on a ground of intersecting highways.

By penetrating deeply into enemy territory, you entered on critical ground.

When you penetrate a small distance, you are on facile ground.

When you come across a place with rough ground behind you and a narrow passage, you are on a hemmed ground.

When entering a region where there is no way for withdrawal, you are on desperate ground.

So:

When you are on dispersive ground, you must unify your troops.

When you are on facile ground, you must keep your troops compacted.

When you are on contentious ground, you must accelerate your defense troops.

When you are on open ground, you must defend your camp carefully.

When you are on ground of intersecting highways, you must form strong alliances with neighboring governments.

When you are on a serious ground, you must ensure the flow of material resources.

When you are on a difficult ground, you must cross it hastily.

When you are on a hemmed ground, you must block access or withdrawal points.

When you are on desperate ground, you have to show your soldiers that there is no choice but to fight to the last man.

The psychology of the soldiers

A commander has to know the psychology of the soldiers:

- They will resist while they are surrounded.
- They will fight desperately while being forced to it.
- They will follow the commander when entering dangerous situations.

Emphasizing

A commander who is unaware of the intentions of neighboring rulers cannot form alliances with them; if he does not know the secrets of the mountains, the dense forests, the dangerous abysses, the precipices, and the swamps, he will not be able to move his troops; if he does not hire native guides, he cannot discover favorable grounds; if he is unaware of the advantages and disadvantages of several battle positions, he cannot command an army serving a sovereign.

If a sovereign's army attacks a strong state, it must not allow this state to gather forces to resist; and wherever such an army goes, it intimidates its enemy and prevents its allies from coming to its aid. So, a state with such an invincible army does not need to seek alliances with other states, nor does it need to establish its power in these states. It only relies on its own forces to intimidate the enemy, capture the enemy's cities, and destroy its state.

If, when leading a sovereign's army, you give rewards independently of customary practice and issue orders independently of what was already agreed, you can command thousands and thousands of horses and men as if you were leading a single man.

Prepare your troops for the operation, but never tell them of your plans; employ them to obtain the advantageous points, but never tell them about the dangers that the disadvantageous situation would entail.

It is only by launching an army into a dangerous position that its soldiers will realize they can survive; only by putting them on desperate ground will they realize they can stay alive. Only when soldiers are placed in danger can they turn defeat into victory.

The success of military operations lies in discovering the enemy's intentions and in the effort to identify its weaknesses.

Concentrate your forces on the enemy, and you can kill its commander, even if he is a thousand *li* away.

This is called "reaching an objective in a cunning and ingenious way."

By declaring war

On the day a declaration of war is decided, you must close all crossings, annul border passes, and end all contact with enemy emissaries. Carefully review your military plans with the temple council and make decisions.

If you discover your opponent's weak point, you have to affect it quickly. Initially capture what is very valuable to the enemy. Do not let the time of your attack be revealed.

Be wise to realize that, to gain victory, your plans must be changed according to the enemy's situation.

At first, assume the purity of a maiden; when the enemy opens the gates to you, attack it as quickly as a skittish hare. In this way, the enemy will be unable to resist you.

Inner part of the Chinese bamboo book of The Art of War ("孫子兵 法"), by Sun Tzu.

CHAPTER XII

火攻

The Attack by Fire

Sun Tzu said:

"There are five ways of attacking with fire. The first is to burn soldiers in their camp; the second is to burn stores; the third is to burn baggage trains; the fourth is to burn arsenals and magazines; the fifth is to hurl dropping fire amongst the enemy."

The attack by fire requires some special care. The favorable time to launch a fire attack is when the weather is dry; the suitable days for setting fire are those when the moon is in the position of the constellations of the Basket of the Winds, the Wall, the Wing, or the Stirrup. Because when the moon is in these positions, strong winds will rise.

In addition, there are five ways to attack with fire. The first is to burn soldiers in their camps; the second is to burn warehouses; the third is to burn supply trains; the fourth is to burn arsenals and powder magazines; and the fifth is to continually throw fire at the enemy.

Illustration from the collection "Heiji Monogatari Emaki" (Museum of Fine Arts, Boston).

Appropriate conduct

When attacking by fire, the fight must be conducted appropriately according to the different situations caused by the five types of attacks by fire.

When the fire reaches the enemy's camp, you must coordinate your action in advance and from the outside. However, when the enemy's camp is on fire and your soldiers are still calm, you should wait and not launch the attack. When the flames gain height, if you manage to cross them, you can attack; if you cannot cross them, remain in your position.

When the fire is set, while you are outside the enemy's camp, you must not enter its limits, but wait for the right moment. If you start the fire before the wind line, never attack against the wind. The wind that blows constantly during the day is likely to calm down at night.

The opportune moment

Any army must know about the different situations regarding the five types of attacks by fire and must continue to wait for the opportune moment.

Thus, a commander who uses fire to support his attack will be sure of victory; the one who uses water to support his attack is strong. Water can block the enemy's advance, but it cannot deprive the enemy of his provisions.

Winning a battle and capturing booty but not consolidating such achievements predicts danger. Because it is a waste of time and effort.

An enlightened sovereign deliberately studies the situation, and a good commander carefully deals with it. If it is not advantageous, never send your troops; if it does not yield you gains, never use your men; if it is not a dangerous situation, never fight a rash battle.

A sovereign must not wage war in an attack of anger and should not send its troops into a moment of indignation. When the situation is favorable to you, take action; when it is unfavorable, do not act. It must be understood that a moment of fury will pass, and the one who is indignant will again be honored, but a state that perishes can never be revived, just as a man who dies can never be resurrected.

The five fire-related developments must be known, the movements of the stars calculated, and an observer placed on the appropriate days.

The one who uses fire as an aid to attack demonstrates intelligence. The one who uses water is capable of increasing its strength. By means of water, an enemy can be intercepted, but it will hardly be defeated.

An enlightened sovereign must direct war affairs with prudence and war with caution. This is the way to keep the state at peace and safety and the army intact.

CHAPTER XIII

用間

The Use of Spies

Sun Tzu said:

"Hostile armies may face each other for years, striving for the victory which is decided in a single day. This being so, to remain in ignorance of the enemy's condition simply because one grudges the outlay of a hundred ounces of silver in honors and emoluments, is the height of inhumanity."

When an army of a hundred thousand men is sent to war a thousand *li* away, the people and the public coffers have to spend a thousand bars of gold every day to support it. There will be internal and external agitations, and many people will wander on the roads. Approximately seven hundred thousand families will be unable to work in the fields.

At this time, eight families formed a community. When a family sent a man to join the army, the seven families contributed to its support. Therefore, when an army of one hundred thousand was mobilized, one hundred thousand families gave their children, and consequently, seven hundred thousand families were responsible for supporting them.

If a commander deludes himself with the granting of superior ranks, honors, and a hundred bars of gold and is unaware of the enemy's situation, he is not a good advisor, and he is not a lord of victory.

If an enlightened sovereign and his commander obtain victory whenever they take action and achieve extraordinary feats, it is because they have prior knowledge and can foresee the unfolding of a war.

This prior knowledge, however, cannot be obtained through ghosts and spirits, nor can based on similar experiences, much less deduced based on calculations of the positions of the sun and the moon. It must be obtained from people who clearly know the enemy's situation.

The commander who knows how to infiltrate spies into enemy cities and villages will soon have many completely devoted people there. He will know, through them, the dispositions of the majority regarding the troops.

These spies will suggest the way and means that should be used to conquer the local population. Thus, when the time comes to carry out the siege, you will be able to win without attacking, without striking a single blow, and without drawing your sword.

Types of spies

There are five types of spies that can be used: local spy, inward spy, converted spy, doomed spy, and surviving spy.

When you employ all five types of spies simultaneously, the enemy cannot discover the methods of operation. It is extremely complicated and becomes a magical weapon for the sovereign to defeat his enemy.

The five types of spies are:

1. Local spies are the enemy's own villagers.

2. Inward spies are the enemy's own employees.

3. Converted spies are the enemy's spies that provide us with information.

4. Doomed spies are our own spies who deliberately obtain false information about our situation and pass it on to the enemy. Normally, they would be caught and sentenced to death.

5. Surviving spies are those that travel between the enemy and us and return with reliable information about the enemy.

How to employ spies

Only the most cunning commander knows how to employ spies.

Only the humanitarian and fair commander knows how to employ spies.

Only the alert and subtle commander knows how to obtain true information from spies.

Really subtle! Truly subtle! There is no place where spying is not possible. If a secret plan is revealed prematurely, the spy and everyone it spoke to will be sentenced to death.

Whoever plans to attack the troops of the enemy or its cities, or assassinate the enemy commander, must first find out the name of the chief of the defense garrison, his aide-de-camp, advisors, sentinels, and bodyguards. Next, it is important to guide your spies to investigate these details.

The strategy consists of finding out the enemy spies that were sent to spy on you. Bribe them, exhort them, and convince them to serve you. They can be converted and will work for your side.

Through these converted spies, you will be capable of obtaining information about the enemy, and you will be able to recruit local spies and inward spies. You must employ your doomed spies to deliver false information about your army to the enemy. In the same way, it is based on this obtained information that our surviving spies will be able to complete their missions at the opportune time.

A sovereign must know how to use the five types of spies. The entire basis of the spying service lies with converted spies; therefore, these must be rewarded generously.

Only the enlightened ruler and the skilled commander, who are capable of recruiting intelligent men as spies, will accomplish great tasks.

The use of spies is essential in war, and the army depends on this service in its movements.

Sun Tzu said:

“The art of war is of vital importance to the State. It is a matter of life and death, a road either to safety or to ruin. Hence it is a subject of inquiry which can on no account be neglected.”

FELICE BEATO